PANKOVIC ANDELKA

TREES & FLOWERS

COLORING BOOK

PUBLISHER: PANKOVIC ANDELKA

To my loveling son and husband

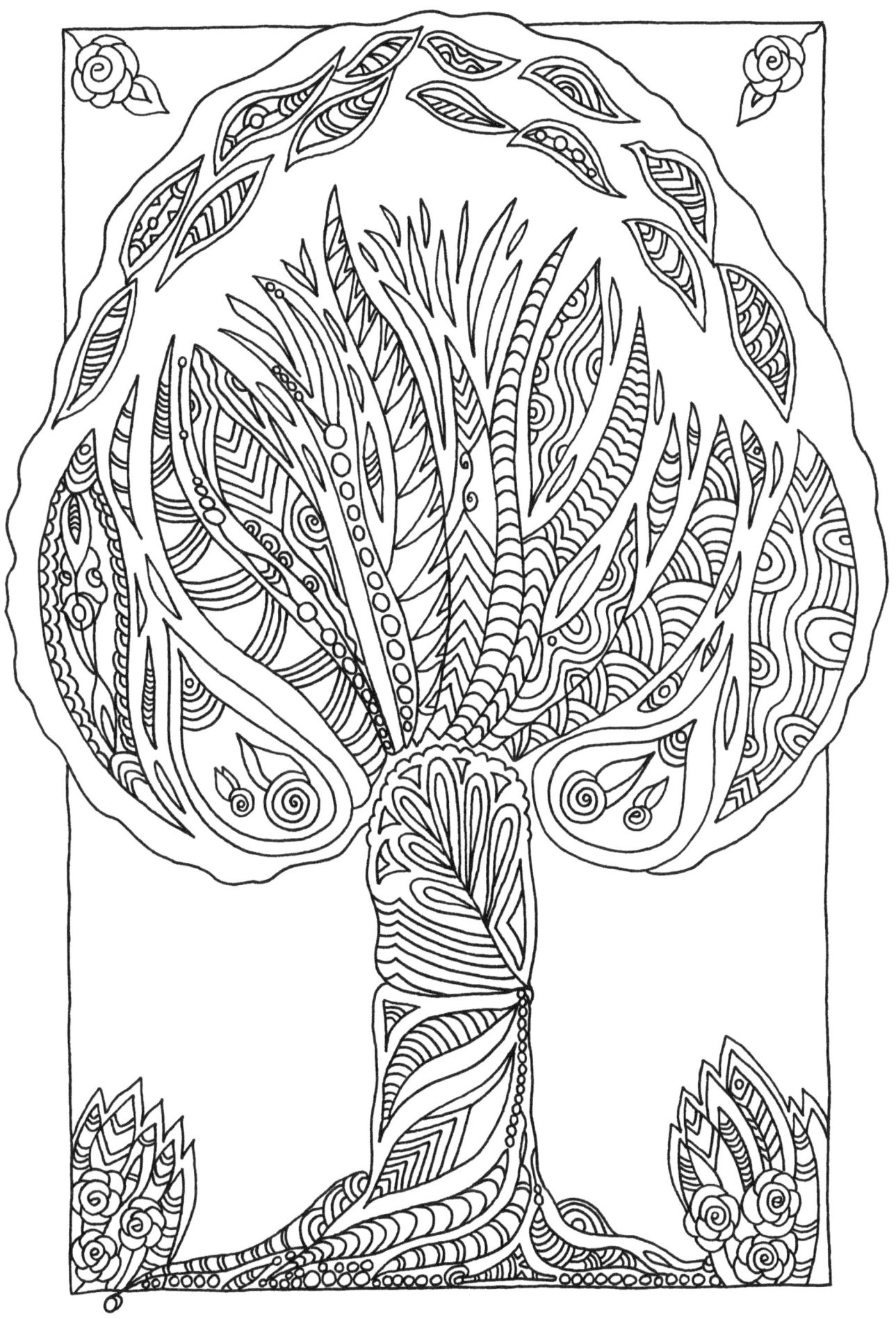

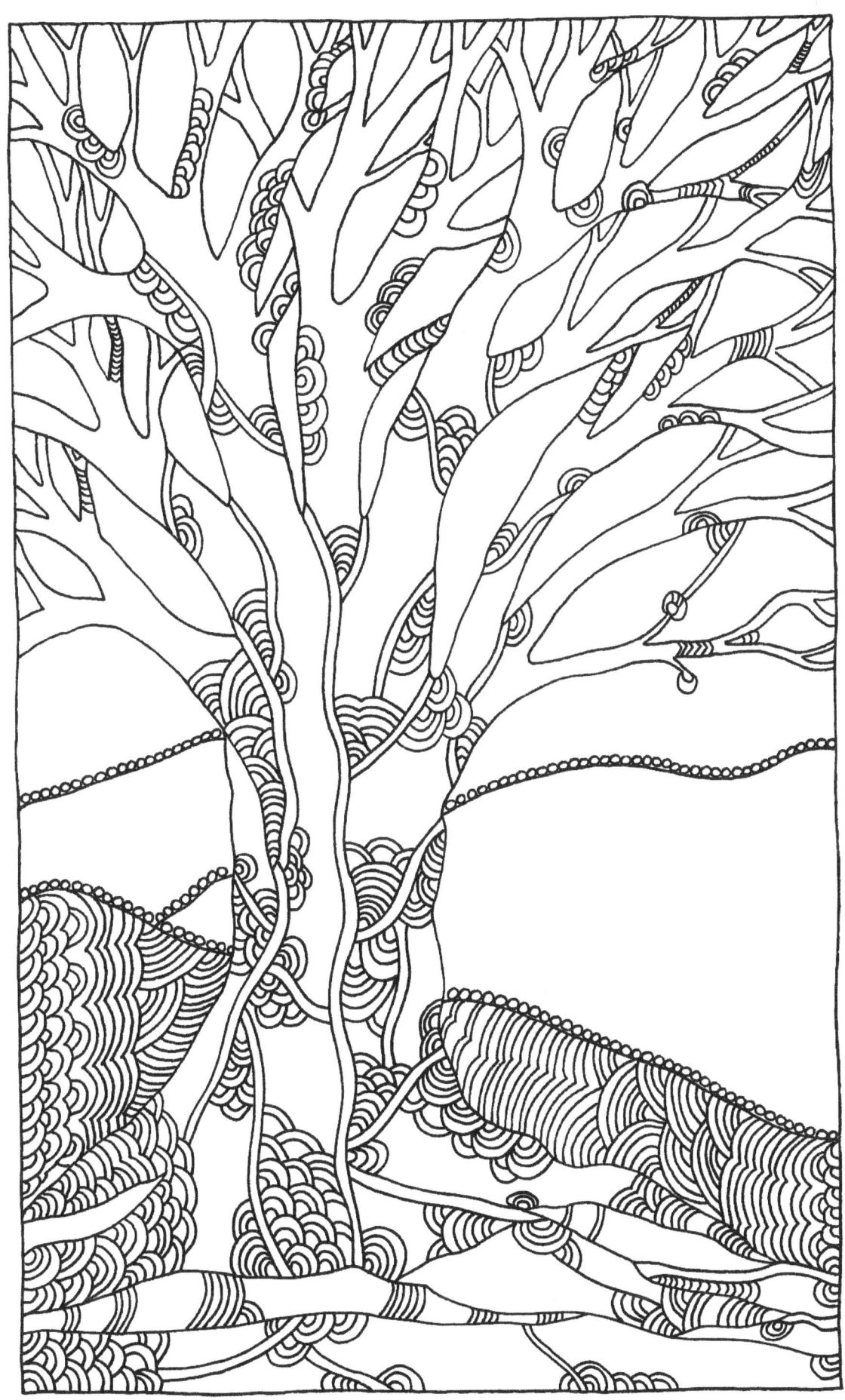

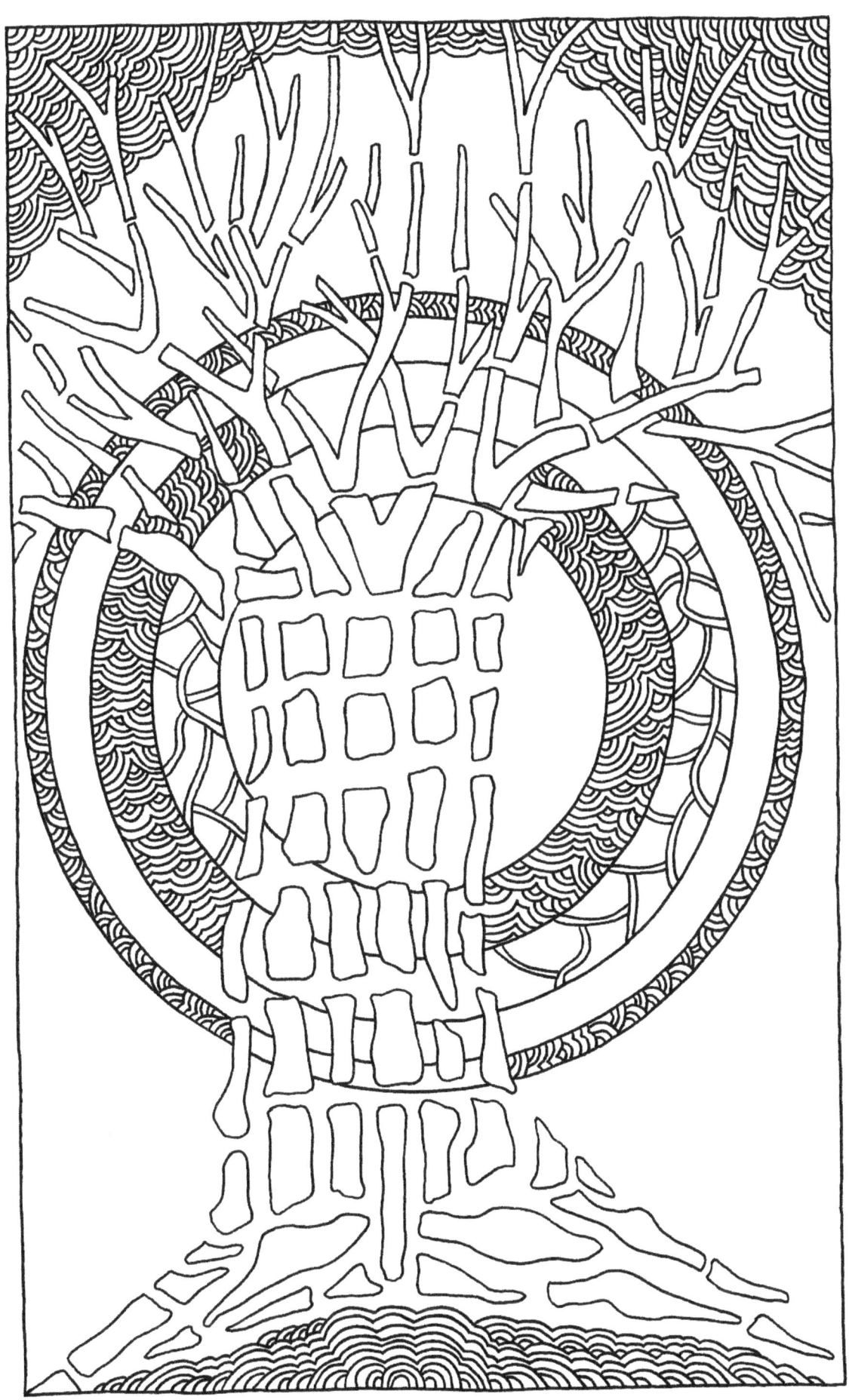

Pankovic Andelka

Born in Belgrade, Serbia, where she lived until 1996. She currently lives in Trieste, Italy. She is married and has a son of 15 years. Degree in geology, still wishing for creative activities, passionate about design.

She is the author of the coloring book Mandala.

www.ingramcontent.com/pod-product-compliance
Lightning Source LLC
Chambersburg PA
CBHW081823280526
45789CB00007B/2323